The Grand Tour Collections
Volume One

Carmen Evans

Pan's Lodge

First published March 2005 by Pan's Lodge,
P.O.Box 300, Waltham Chase, Hampshire, SO32 2WN

in an edition of 500 copies, of which:
20 copies, numbered 1 – 20, are for collaborators on the publication
480 copies, numbered 21 – 500, are for general sale.

This copy is no.

Photography and Art Direction: Carmen Evans

Text: Carmen Evans

Design, Artwork and Illustrations: Clare Upton

Proof Reading: Brackley Proofreading Services

Printed and bound in UK by Kent Edwards Ltd

ISBN 0 9549792 0 6

The publisher would like to thank the following who supplied additional photography:
Jason Meneely: p8, p12

FRONT COVER DETAIL The Turkish Tent carved from Limewood by Ian G. Brennan

Returned from the Grand Tour, and inspired by scenes of classical antiquity, the eighteenth-century landowner took to remodelling his parkland with great collections of ruins, eye-catchers and monuments. Within the parkland canvas these adornments are portrayed as an arena in which he could house his burgeoning collection of art, antiquities and curiosities, accumulated whilst undertaking the Grand Tour.

Through a series of enchanting landscape pictures, we discover the picturesque views, and architectural delights that we will encounter on our tour of the eighteenth-century parkland. We catch a glimpse of an exotic tent and a monumental spire reflected in the crystal waters of the serpentine lake; whilst descending the open, grassy banks, towards the cascade, we sight a shell-encrusted pavilion and ruined arch, screened by a group of evergreen trees. Continuing along the meandering trail, we notice the temple flag sailing high above the tree-tops, before turning to discover the deciduous tree-lined approach that will lead us to the Gothic Library.

The pineapple symbolised the landowner's penchant for incorporating **great botanical collections**, imported from foreign lands, into his sweeping parkland canvas.

Away from the grassy banks of the serpentine lake, the fragments of an old, pebble path draw us into the dark, wooded depths of the parkland. Nestled deep within the ancient trees of Seven-Oaks Lawn, the diffused sunlight that filters through the overhead trees reveals the intricately patterned walls of the Shell House.

The Shell House

...fragments of an old,
pebble path...

Built as a conspicuous display of the landowner's wealth and taste, the Shell House exemplified the eighteenth century's taste for collecting the exotic and rare. Sir George Staunton fashioned his parkland adornment upon the design of th Chichester Cross;

with hexagonal walls and deep stone buttresses, its ornamental flint and shell-work decoration would have drawn upon the boundless resources of his natural history collections.

Vast quantities of shells would have been used to embellish the paths, specimens imported from foreign lands.

encrust the walls, and furnish its interior, with new and exotic

One such renowned female proponent of decorative shell work was Mrs Mary Delany (1700-88) who advised upon many important Shell Houses within the eighteenth-century parkland. As an avid collector, she sought to use commonplace shells for ornamentation, whilst incorporating only exotic and rare specimens into her acclaimed collections. This categorical method was often employed within the Shell House, whereby shells were used as both decorative material and treasured exhibit.

Attributed to the landowner's wife and daughters, the collection and decorative embellishment of the Shell House became an accepted and fashionable pastime for the refined, eighteenth-century lady. Her presence could often be felt intertwined with the landowner's burgeoning collection of natural history finds. Often used as a pavilion for light refreshment or entertainment, its custom-designed furniture and furnishings drew upon the stylised, whorling patterns of the Rococo movement – contributing a sense of feminine frivolity to the landowner's collection of parkland adornments.

Sir George Staunton noted in his inventory that some thirty-six items were housed within the Shell House: shells, mineral, roman pottery, a stuffed crocodile and a toucan's bill, formed part of his eclectic and widely-sourced anthology of the natural world.

Enriched with natural collections of **shell, stone and coral**, the Shell House provided a fitting backdrop in which the landowner could house the **curiosities and collections** he had accumulated whilst undertaking the Grand Tour.

The Roman Mausoleum

...shrouded by the dark,
symbolic plantings of yew
and evergreen...

Stood upon a tessellated stone floor, an **ornamental urn** is framed by the ruined archway – as depicted within The Mausoleum painting, by William Hannan, 1773.

Within the roofless internal chambers of the triumphal arch, the prevalent sense of decay and melancholy was heightened by Hamilton's collection of ancient artefacts; a cluttered array of Roman busts, columns, capitals, urns and relics were once housed within its dank chambers and niches.

The Roman Mausoleum views captured by William Hannan, and the illustrative scenes upon Wedgwood and Bentley's Green Frog Service, revealed an imposing arch that joined the two chambers of the Mausoleum.

Portrayed in a ruined, abandoned state, a section of the representational arch, strewn with fallen leaves and ivy tendrils, unveils its decorative soffit, with trompe l'oeil carved roses set within square, coffered panels.

Upon encountering the Mausoleum, we can take the symbolic passage through the ruined arch, leaving behind the dark, melancholic scenery of mortal life, into the pastoral setting of the arcadian world beyond. The lush, verdant pastures, distant hanging wood and the meandering River Mole typified the eighteenth century's vision and interpretation of an arcadian world within the parkland canvas.

The symbolic inclusion of the Roman Mausoleum, within the parkland collections, delivers a solemn message about mortality. Contrary to this philosophical message, the permanence of the triumphal arch ensures the perpetual presence of the landowner across his parkland canvas.

The landowner's **architectural collection** would not be complete without the obligatory **temple**, and so it is in pursuit of this classical edifice that we set off towards the northern part of parkland known as Beacon Lawn.

Reminiscent of the **classical architecture** studied during the Grand Tour, the quintessential temple highlighted the eighteenth-century's fondness for collecting and incorporating formal, classical architecture into the parkland canvas; an assortment of European-inspired **arches, bridges, obelisks and temples** imitated the archetypal buildings epitomised in the landscape paintings of Claude Lorraine and Nicolas Poussin.

The Temple

...an ancestral flag sailed
high above the tree-tops...

From behind the Doric base, an indigenous pheasant reminds us of the naturalistic setting in which the classical temple and memorial urn are situated within the parkland.

Resplendent against the temple's **weathered stone columns**, the memorial urn is a magnificent example of the Etruscan vases collected by the eighteenth-century landowner during his Grand Tour. With fine classical details – **grape vine garlands, acanthus leaf handles and gilt accents** – its ornamentation was typical of the venerated ancient European style.

High above the grassy banks of the hanging wood, the glistening rays cast by a gold crescent finial draw our attention, across the sweeping parkland, towards the exotic, architectural delight known as the Turkish Tent.

The Turkish Tent

...the glistening rays cast
by a gold crescent finial...

As an architectural exponent of the English Parkland abroad, the Turkish Tent is an appropriate building in which to house the representational dinner service of Empress Catherine of all the Russias.

Framed by the grandiose, festooned opening of the tent, a magnificent banquet table, dressed in trompe l'oeil swathes of fabric, bullion and tassels, complements the theatrical decorations that furnish the front façade of the Turkish Tent.

The banquet table displays a collection of elaborately decorated dinner plates that epitomise the legendary dinner service, known as the Green Frog Service, commissioned by Empress Catherine from Wedgwood and Bentley in 1773. The great dinner service, much associated with the history and depiction of the eighteenth-century landscape, was an unparalleled repertory of picturesque landscape views, including numerous scenes at Painshill Park, illustrated upon 944 individual pieces of Wedgwood creamware.

As a pictorial account of the English Parkland, the Green Frog Service illustrated a great collection of parkland adornments: ruins, eye-catchers, pavilions, temples, grottoes, mausoleums and monuments.

These archetypal embellishments were depicted within the context of the parkland canvas, and, as picturesque views, were framed by trailing ivy tendrils, surmounted by the crest of a green frog.

Amidst the ivy garlands a small, ornamental frog suggests the distinguished crest that decorated the dinner service designed specifically for the Chesmenski Palace, situated in an area known as the Frog-Marsh, near Leningrad.

This celebrated dinner service has, within its framing ivy tendrils, immortalised and commemorated the architectural collections that have enriched the eighteenth-century parkland canvas.

The landowner, Beware Chalk Pit and a fox portray

ne original tale that surrounds this monument.

Set within the **naturalistic scenery** of Mount Down, a landscape picture portraying the landowner and Beware Chalk Pit is reminiscent of the paintings by artist Sawrey Gilpin (1733-1807), who as an accomplished painter of horses, with their owners, incorporated **wild, dramatic landscapes** into his work.

Dedicated to the landowner's prize horse, this monumental pyramid, **rising high above its equine tomb**, typified a popular addition to the eighteenth-century landscape. Its inclusion within the architectural collections is a conscious symbol of the **landowner's enduring presence** within the parkland canvas.

As we stand upon Mount Down, looking **back across the sweeping parkland** canvas, we realise that we have simply begun our journey through the Grand Tour Collections that adorn the landowner's glorious masterpiece...

Author's Acknowledgments

With special thanks to the following historic Parks, who have allowed me into their gardens to photograph, without their support and enthusiasm this book would not have been possible.

Farley Mount Country Park
Crab Wood Depot, Sarum Road
Winchester, Hampshire SO22 5QS
Telephone: 01962 860 948

Painshill Park
Portsmouth Road, Cobham
Surrey KT11 1JE
Telephone: 01932 868 113

Staunton Country Park
Middle Park Way
Havant, Hampshire PO9 5HB
Telephone: 02392 453 405

I would like to thank the many people who have freely given their time, support and expertise to this project, in particular Clare Upton whose beautiful artwork and illustrations have perfectly interpreted my original ideas; Ray Meneely, Emma Womar and Ian Pringle for their help in-front and behind the camera; David Berry for the generous supply of furnishings from his showrooms; Caroline Gorton for her early encouragement; my partner Jason for creating the many props featured, and my parents for their constant support over the past four years.

The Author would also like to thank the following companies and individuals who have supplied the many specialised furnishings and artifacts that feature in this book:

Brunschwig & Fils
10 The Chambers
Chelsea Harbour
Design Centre
London SW10 0XF
Tel: 0207 351 5797

Edward Harpley
Crownings
Brettenham, Ipswich
Suffolk IP7 7PA
Tel: 01449 737 999

Hampshire Riding
Therapy Centre Ltd
Hensting Lane
Fishers Pond
Eastleigh
Hants SO50 7HH
Tel: 01962 777 714

Harrison & Gil
7 Wessex Trade Centre
Ringwood Road
Parkstone, Poole
Dorset BH12 3PF
Tel: 01202 717 017

Ian G. Brennan
Sculptor
www.britishsculptor.com

Individual Interior Design
132 Stockbridge Road
Winchester
Hants SO22 6RN
Tel: 01962 855 165

Langford Antiques
70 Albert Road
Southsea
Hants PO5 2SL
Tel: 02392 830 517

Maitland-Smith
G. & M. Thomson Ltd
89 Richford St
London W6 7HJ
Tel: 0208 743 9588

Ornamenta Ltd
23 South Terrace
South Kensington
London SW7 2TB
Tel: 0207 591 0077

Pierre Frey Ltd
251-253 Fulham Road
London SW3 6HY
Tel: 0207 376 5599

Tenterden House Interiors
4 West Cross
Tenterden
Kent TN30 6JL
Tel: 01580 764 481

Theodore Alexander Ltd
Chapel Hill
Kingsclere Road
Basingstoke
Hants RG21 5UQ
Tel: 01256 406 200

Wendy Cushing Trimmings
G7 Chelsea Harbour
Design Centre
London SW10 0XE
Tel: 0207 351 5796

Zoffany
G9 Chelsea Harbour
Design Centre
London SW10 0XE
Tel: 0207 349 0043